# Purely Pointless Primitive Poetry

Cameron Tinson

BookLeaf
Publishing

Presentation by *BookLeaf Publishing*

Web: www.bookleafpub.com

E-mail: info@bookleafpub.com

ISBN: 978-93-95755-62-7

First edition 2022

*I dedicate this book to Nicole. Without you I would never have found this opportunity to get my foot in the door and put myself out there. Thank you.*

# PREFACE

This book is full of amateur poetry organised to start with chaos but improve as the pages progress. Stick with it and you will not only gain a deeper understanding of my mind but you will feel a sense of calm as the beat of the poems slowly become more steady and clear, itching those OCD tendencies that go crazy at the start.

# The Perfect Storm

I live with no life,
Sad, empty, and wasted.
Unable to remember
My actions are often hasted.

One choice made quickly,
The largest of them all.
To accept and to care,
You came along, quite small.

Through thick and thin,
You've always been there.
Even when my heart,
Has appeared quite bare.

I truly do wish
I could've been more for you.
I gave far too little
That much i know, is true,

You don't seem to mind,
You excite all the same.
Listening and hearing
Every mention of your name.

Though I've been absent

The first half of your life.
I blame it all
On false things I call strife.

From this day forth
You're more than my world.
How could you not be
When you're my little girl.

I'll give you more attention
Focusing on you'll be my norm.
I love you my girl,
My Gorgeous, Perfect Storm.

# Cameron's Creative Crap

Crazy clinics control caring clients
As angels attend, analysing abilities
Managing mystics, magic, muscle material,
Edging effortlessly every evening, emptying
Rancid roles, reporting reckless races
Over obnoxious opinions, overcoming orders
Nicknaming naive, nerdy names naturally.

Together terrible town types technically
Immortalise intense, idiotic inevitabilities inside
Nature noisily negotiating nomenclature
naturally
Suddenly seeing societal supplies seriously
Owing organisations opportunities only
obsessively
Nagging networks notioning nervous nerds.

# Angels and Demons

Should I message her?
No, that would show desperation, and I don't want to appear desperate.
But what if she wants me to message? Perhaps to feel wanted and appreciated?
And smothered, and bothered, and gasping for air from this suffocation.
Well Maybe I can just message a friend instead?
Yes, my friend has known me for many years, they won't feel smothered.
Except I already messaged that friend hours ago. And no response? They obviously don't care for me.
Perhaps they are just busy? Maybe they can't check their messages yet?
Of course they can. I've seen their daily schedule. They practically live on their phone.
Well perhaps I should just message someone else?
I have plenty of friends I can message.
But no others that care for me. No-one really wants to talk with me.
Of course I have others, if they didn't care for me then why would I consider them my friend?

Because I'm desperate, because I fear loneliness and rejection.
I'm just going to message another friend.
But that friend doesn't really care for me.
Think about it, when was the last time I just talked about nothing with them?
We just have a different relationship to most people.
They just care in a different way.
Or maybe they're just using me to entertain them.
That's why we only talk when we're playing games or when they want something from me.
Maybe I shouldn't message anyone then?
That's ok, I don't really need to rely on others for my own happiness.
I can just sit down and watch a movie, or play a game.
Except that I've been doing that for the last few hours.
I'm obviously not enjoying that otherwise I wouldn't even think about stopping doing it.
But of course I would think about stopping it.
What is life without a little variety?
What else can I do if I can't be with someone or on my own?
Find myself elsewhere. Maybe I'm just upset because I wish to learn, wish to broaden that mind of mine?

If I really wanted to be smart though, I would
have tried harder in school.
I would have made something of myself by now.
Ah, but not everyone can achieve what they
want that early in life, for life is more nuanced
than that.
So I have a nuanced life? My life isn't straight
forward?
Of course I have a nuanced life.
How else can one live but with the subtleties of
upbringing and varied amounts of personal
growth?
So should I continue to learn?
Should I continue to find the rabbit holes of
knowledge and learn new things?
Indeed it is best, if that is what will make me
happy.
But what if I try and fail? Will it make me happy
to know that I'm a failure?
At least I would have tried. I can't succeed if I
do not allow a chance to fail.
Then I shall try. I will probably fail, but at least I
will grow, even from the failure.

# The Doll House

A porcelain doll in a lego house, one designed to
keep it safe
Every crack that appears in the doll creates
another room
Each room makes the lego house bigger and
heavier
Though the house cares not for it's size or
maintenance
So long as the porcelain never breaks and is
always fixed.
The doll made of fragile materials is not able to
support the room
Is not created to hold up a roof or hold back a
wall
What happens then when the wall caves in or a
room breaks down?
The doll, wishing not to break, leaves the lego
house to crumble.
The doll may stand within the broken room
applying tape to the cracks
But they both know that these fixes are
temporary
Knowing that tape can't actually fix the wall
The moment the house reaches for the assistance
of the super glue

Cracks start appearing within the porcelain once again
Building another room onto the lego house.

# Finding Yourself

Desperation is not a pretty look.
When feeling it try your best to hide it,
Be alone again, build your own handbook.

Everyone reads you like an open book.
They can see inside and see past your mask,
Desperation is not a pretty look.

Learn a new skill, try that class your friend took.
Become one with yourself, learn to embrace,
Be alone again, build your own handbook.

It is hard at first, your heart will be shook.
Keep telling yourself, like it's a mantra,
Desperation is not a pretty look.

Take some time away and sit by a brook,
Bring some paper and a pen, sit and write.
Be alone again, build your own handbook.

Once you know yourself you'll find your own
hook,
And title the front like you know you should.
Desperation is not a pretty look.
Be alone again, build your own handbook.

# ADHD Be Like

Like catching a ball that disappears the moment
it's in your grasp,
As aggressive as a hornet, you'll find it is
randomly biassed,
It holds back thoughts and makes you
acclimatised to adding addictions,
So controlling you would think it's a politician,
taking control of your life.

Some hyperfocus, some hypofocus, others like
me jump around,
Not able to focus on any one thing but still
performing the one activity like there is no
others,
Like this game, then a week later that game, a
week goes by before a different activity,
Making me a mild master moving on and
missing maintenance.

Learning new skills better than the majority as
quickly as a bird learns to fly,
Though leaving almost every activity just about
as quickly as it was started,

# Ball Brain

Living my life as a creature that's quite small.
I have loved you my whole life and given you
my all.
You're trying to be slick,
Time for you to be quick,
Just hurry up and throw the damn ball!

# Reigan the Vegan

We may not agree on all we think,
Though we love each other all the same.
The love one would feel for a brother or sister,
You hold me up like a candle to a flame.

You assist with life, and keep my mind sound,
We converse and discuss the way some would
debate.
Not trying to change each other's mind,
But exploring ideas with no reasons to berate.

You care for the environment, me not so much,
I can't give up my meat, even though you're
vegan.
I must say to you my good, dear, friend,
I really am glad to have moved and met you,
Reigan.

# The Walks

We came together and clicked all too well,
Who would have thought it would not last so
long.
We'd go on a walk, and talk for a spell,
And nothing ever felt like it was wrong.

Five times, six times, often more every week,
I loved life, I loved you, and all we did.
We would walk to the store, or down the creek,
We knew this place like a map on a grid.

Until He came along and stopped all that,
Didn't notice at first, quick though, it's true.
Should have taken that as a caveat,
And fought much harder to keep up with you.

You walked every day, walks slowly got long.
But he stays home, not often going out,
Your walks disappeared, and that was just
wrong,
Not long before walks turned into a drought.

That all happened quite a long time ago,
And now things are starting to look better.
When you go for your walks you look aglow,

Through repetition you'll drop these fetters.

Now you walk most days and you also dance,
You are growing your strength with so much grace.
You're finally starting to take a stance,
Soon you'll be able to finish your race.

# Quickly Descending

Disaster always strikes around you it would
seem,
A twisted form of reality, almost like a dream.
Very intense is your life, but living all the same,
In and out of consciousness, like life is a game.
Daily you're out, living at one extreme.

Where will you go and when will it end?
Every clear day you pass gets you back on the
mend.

Can you really live life if you can't see around?
A shuttle like you, quickly becoming
earthbound.
Resetting parachute, the buttons they mash.
Everything they can try, right before they crash.

# The Majestic Boar

Like a boar there is anger and not coming slow,
The boar rushes to attack, caring not for reason.
Be it summer or winter, autumn or spring,
The anger it shows doesn't care 'bout season.

You can try to argue, you can try to explain,
A boar doesn't care as it does its own thing.
They live their own life and don't listen at all,
They live by their own rules, they think that
they're king.

Though I would argue that a boar's not the best,
If you want to be on top, go and be a bear
instead.
A bear is strong, and can fend for itself,
A bear knows that strength is all in the head.

A bear sits and watches and listens around,
They decide on the spot whether to play or to
fight.
Everyone knows not to mess with the bears,
The Russians, however, hang out for the night.

So I wish you would change and listen to reason,
Like a bear, not a boar, I want you to listen.

I think that they're great, but boars should evolve,
Change to a bear and like gold you will glisten.

# The Grey Pup

A puppy you were, a puppy you'll be,
I will always think "you're a puppy to me."
Though you're getting older, the grey coming
back,
When it comes to playing ball you'll always
have the knack.
You're twelve years old, but what can I say?
Now that you're tracked you'll never get away.

Run, jump, and play. I wish you the best,
You've kept up your energy, for that I'm
impressed.
Perhaps that was me, perhaps it's just you,
You still outrun most others, now that much is
true.
You just keep on going, not knowing when to
stop,
You run and run and run, until you literally drop.

You started as a pet, now a member of the house,
Everyone 'round here, they all think that you're
grouse.
Though you're scared of TV and I can't fathom
why,

When it gets turned on you can't turn a blind
eye.
You Run and you hide, often under the chair,
I'll teach you not to fear it, this I do swear.


Twelve years old, but still not feeling old,
You learn very well, still doing what you're told.
We give you treats and teach you tricks,
That saying about old dogs, with you it doesn't
mix.
You like learning new things, you really are fine,
At the end of the day, I'm glad you are mine.

# No Competition

Why you like that? Why not change that?
Why you walking over her like a doormat?
Why allow this? Why take this?
Been watching you drop down the abyss.
It's not normal, it's paranormal,
The way you treat each other's so informal.
You talk smack, she yells back,
Then perpetuate each other's negative feedback.

Why can't you guys see the pain,
Like standing outside in the rain.
Trying to bring the other down,
Just so you can wear the crown.

Loading munitions, like it's your mission,
Treating love like it's a competition.
You try to smother, one another,
Instead of taking care of the other.
It hurts you, I know it's true,
Twisting into one another like a corkscrew.
You both lament, you both resent,
Living life in a state of constant torment.

You say the other is the one,
And that is why you do not run,

That's fine just go and break the spell,
And start treating each other well.

Don't be snappy, it may sound sappy,
But just try to make the other really happy.
Show devotion, share emotions,
Go and show the other one that you're well
chosen.
And if you dare, show that you care,
Put all your love in the open air.
Life can be great, it's not too late,
Just go to the other and captivate.

# THAT guy

There once was a guy from school,
Who always liked acting like a tool,
He would have a lot of fun,
By behaving quite dumb,
I told him "I love you, but you're a fool."

# The Fog

At the maze of the mind I stand at the edge.
I try peering in, staring over that ledge.

Is it smoke, cloud, or gas that fills my meadow
of dreams?
If I wish to see past I must go to extremes.

I want to see the sun and see all that it lights.
So I can bring myself up to incredible heights.

It may be hard now but I will worry no more,
For one day they'll all hear the sound of my roar.

I will blow that fog far with all of my breath
So that I may live well till the time of my death.

# Is Greed Good?

Stock and Crypto, there's no need to tip-toe
You make me feel like someone out there cares,
You were found, to you I'm bound
A member of a race that belongs in pairs.

The feeling was quick, though I've never been
slick
With you there's just no need,
You don't call me honey, you think about money
With just the right amount of greed.

You teach me some, knowing I'm not dumb
You've broadened my horizon,
You let me be me, you obviously see
With our personalities there's no compromisin'.

So let's keep going, let's keep showing
That we're there for the other,
I will always be in touch, but hopefully not too
much
The last thing I want is to smother.

I really hope this slippery slope
Will end up going well.
Unlike the rest you seem the best
Please don't toll my knell.

# Loving Ghosts

We love you and you love us but what can I say?
It really hurts us greatly when you get up and
run away.

You've done it before, you'll do it again, but that
which hurts the most,
When you run, and when you hide, you really
are a ghost.

You go, we chase, you disappear, we call your
name for ages,
The grief we feel when you're not here comes
and goes in stages.

At first we worry 'cause you are gone, we're
scared you won't come back,
But stage two comes, we know your past, we
decide to cut some slack.

We wait a day, a little more, and panik when
stage three starts,
We hope you find your way back home, from the
bottom of our hearts.

You come on back and walk on in as if you were
always here,
But when we see you with us again, we always
go and cheer.

Sometimes though, you don't come back,
instead you are found,
We're lucky that no harm comes to you because
you really get around.

So please do me a favour and please don't run
away,
Because we love you and you love us so what
else can I say?

# Lessons Go Both Ways

Depression and anxiety, not really much variety,
You always told me if they existed you would
really have them.
I'm telling you, this must be true, you always
swear it black and blue,
Your misbelief in a damaged brain has caused
you grief and mayhem.

Over the years, not switching gears, I was trying
to fight your fears,
"You're not depressed just being lazy," is
something that you told me.
I wish that when you said that that it did not
make me feel real flat,
I just pushed through and tried to live and be as
free as I could be.

I knew you cared, you were not spared, it was a
cross you had to bare,
Though at the time I did not listen I knew that I
was different.
You tried your best, I did protest, though not
unstressed you have progressed,
I'm sure that it was not easy, I must have been
vociferant.

But nowadays we get along, your love has made
me strong,
Perhaps you thought that I was right and sought
to make your life greater.
You're travelling around the Earth and showing
what your life is worth,
I wonder if you will be able to travel the equator.

This poem's hard, but you taught grit, by saying
I should never quit,
Even when I think that everything I do is really
quite dumb.
So if I may, I have to say, that at the end of every
day,
When I'm asked by any other people, I really
love my Mum.

# Ups and Downs

Up
…
Down
…
Up
Life feels great,
Down
But you know that it's bait.
Up
Leading all the way to fun,
Down
But only when you're done.
Up
With activities for the day,
Down
For which you must pay.
Up
You get what you pay for,
Up
So you do the things you adore,
Up
Feeling good to your core,
Down
Only until your next score.
Down

So you chase that hit,
Down
Even though you won't admit,
Down
Feeling like a misfit,
Up
Tell yourself you won't quit.
Up
You try your hardest and you try,
Up
Successes looking you in the eye,
Up
Tell your friends and imply,
Up
Demystify when you spy,
Up
The reasons as to why,
Up
Always ending up on a high.
Up
…
Up
…

# Time Dilation

Sitting and waiting is a hard thing to do,
Like in the dusk with my morning brew.
I hate to stop, I like to go,
I hate the experience when life is slow.

Time is subjective or so they say,
I guess that's why I have the longest day.
Regularly I'm bored out of my brain,
I often feel that I'm going insane.

But then there's the times I sit down to watch,
Wanting a minute, the timing I botch.
It feels like not long but ends up at night,
I really hate that I'm losing my light

I need to move, to groove, lots to prove,
But this time dilation I wish to remove.
To stop is to hurt, to go is to push,
Ignoring the people saying to shush.

They don't understand these thoughts in my
head,
How hard it can be in this water I tread.
But soon they'll get it, they will understand,
Assuming that everything goes as planned.

My meds will kick in, I soon will improve,
My mood will be stable, my actions behoove.
They will see what I was, and what I can be,
And finally my mind will let me be me.

# Lessons From Above

Gaming buddy, finance study, father, friend,
that's you,
You've always told me, tried to mould me, as
one part of your crew.

We'd play some crib, you'd cook some rib, we'd
sit down at your table,
You'd have some fun, by telling one of your
many fables.

You'd make your bids, and tell us kids, it's us
versus the planet,
Gave up your scotch, so you could watch, your
look as hard as granite.

Now it's been years since you've had beers, you
really are a star,
And now you show that wealth can grow even
when you're quite bizarre.

You've taught a lot, I'll shoot my shot, and hope
it works out well,
It's never known until you're grown, where
happiness can dwell.

So thank you sir, I must concur, your lessons
may have been tough,
But in this life, push through the strife, for sure
you taught enough.